The SPACE CADET and the MARIONETTE

Helen Meinardi Stearns
Illustrated by Clara Urbahn

Cricketfield Press
Camden, Maine

Copyright © 1986 by Helen M. Stearns
ISBN 0-9614281-2-0
All rights reserved

Printed by Camden Printing
Color design by Searls Design, Inc.
Music arranged by Sandra P. Jerome
Binding by New Hampshire Bindery

The Space Cadet and the Marionette

To All Young Readers —

Knowing how much you enjoy coloring books, I have left most of the pictures in this one for you to use your imagination on.

Have fun —

Helen Meinardi Stearns

The Space Cadet and the Marionette

A space ca- det

and a mar- i- on- ette

JASON

are the talk of the nurs- 'ry room.

It was plain to see from the mo-ment they met
Their lit- tle doll hearts went
boom, boom, boom!

Now he takes her
up on trips to the moon

And she's teach- ing him to dance.

JASON
THE TALKING RABBIT
THE TALKING RABBIT
CARROT HOUSE

But the oth- er toys in the nurs- 'ry room
are wise to their big ro- mance.

Late at night aft- er Ba- by's a- sleep
And it's time for the toy- land jam- bo- ree

They both come to life and go sail- ing a- way
To stroll hand in hand on the Milk- y Way;

or if it's bad weath- er, they sneak off to- geth- er

To kiss in the dark
in their make- be- lieve park.

5

Oh, there's love in bloom in the nurs- 'ry room,
And most ev- 'ry one's will- ing to bet
5
2
5
5
2
5

That soon these two
will be bride and groom

The ca- det and his mar- i- on- ette.

The Space Cadet and the Marionette

D G D
They both come to life and go sail- ing a- way To stroll hand in hand on the
G7 C D
Milk- y Way; or if it's bad weath- er, they sneak off to- geth- er To kiss in
C G7
the dark in their make- be- lieve park. Oh, there's love in bloom in the nurs- 'ry room,
C G7 C
And most ev- 'ry one's will- ing to bet That soon these two will be bride
F G7 C
and groom The ca- det and his mar- i- on- ette.

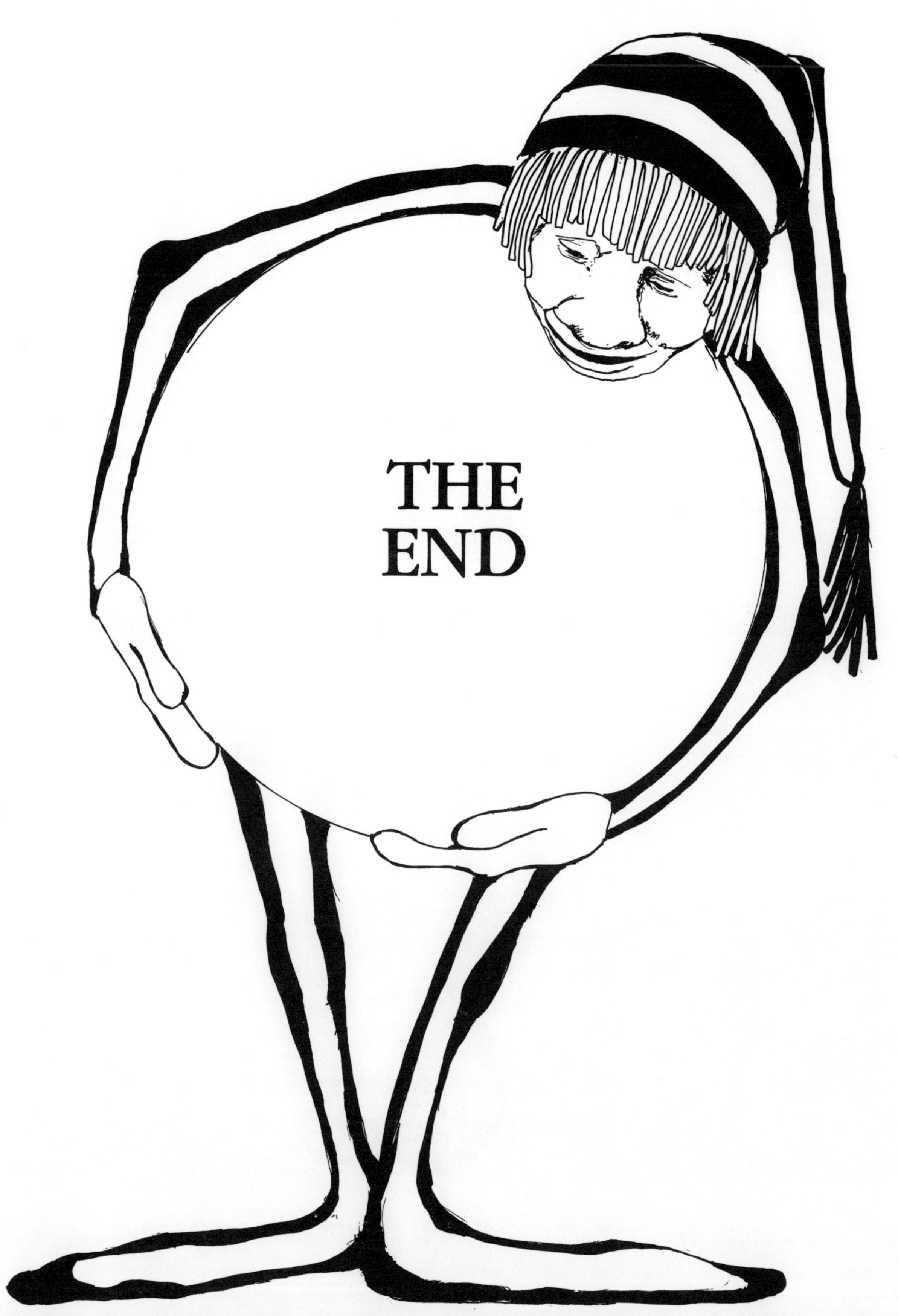
THE
END

ACKNOWLEDGMENTS

Special thanks to my friend Kathy Brandes of Wordsworth Editorial Service for her expert advice and encouragement.

To the Village Shop staff for their creative secretarial help.

To Bill White for his usual fine typesetting.

Camden, Maine